Series 561

The First
Queen
Elizabeth

by L DU GARDE PEACH OBE MA PhD D Litt
with illustrations by JOHN KENNEY

Ladybird Books Loughborough

The Story of the First
QUEEN ELIZABETH

On a fine Sunday in the late summer of the year 1533, more than four hundred years ago, a baby girl was born in a palace at Greenwich on the River Thames, between London and the sea.

Her parents were the King and Queen of England, Henry VIII and Anne Boleyn, the daughter of an Alderman of the City of London.

The child was christened Elizabeth. Her father and mother, who were disappointed because she was not a boy, did not know that she was to rule over England as one of the greatest Queens ever to sit on the English Throne.

King Henry VIII had been married before, and Elizabeth had an elder sister named Mary. Mary was sixteen years older than Elizabeth, and was a very different kind of person. She was to cause Elizabeth much trouble and unhappiness when they both grew up.

Mary became Queen of England when Elizabeth was twenty years old, and at first she was kind to her.

English people at that time were divided into Catholics and Protestants. Both were Christians, but they attended different kinds of churches.

Queen Mary was a Catholic. What was more, she was married to King Philip II of Spain. The English people hated the Spaniards, and the Protestants disliked Mary because she was a Catholic. Consequently there were many people who were plotting to put Elizabeth on the throne instead of Mary.

Mary believed that Elizabeth was involved in these plots, and it is indeed quite possible that she was. So Mary had her sister arrested and imprisoned in the Tower of London.

This was a very grim experience for a young princess who was only twenty years of age.

Mary tried hard to prove that Elizabeth was guilty of plotting to seize her throne, but Elizabeth was very clever and was able to answer the charges against her. She did this so well that many people said she ought not to be kept in the Tower any longer, so Mary was forced to set her free.

This did not mean that Elizabeth was free to go where she liked. Mary was afraid that there might be more plots to make Elizabeth Queen of England, so she sent her to live at a place called Hatfield.

Here Elizabeth lived quietly for nearly four years. She spent her time in learning Latin and Greek, and she became one of the best scholars in England. She also had a very clever man to advise her. This was Sir William Cecil, who was afterwards to play a great part in the history of England.

Elizabeth's life was not an easy one during the reign of her sister Mary. It was not even safe. Mary was a strange woman who sometimes seemed to be very fond of her young sister, but at other times bitterly accused her of things of which she was innocent.

Most of all, Mary was angry with Elizabeth because she believed she was a Protestant. Mary wanted England to remain a Catholic country, and was afraid that when Elizabeth came to the throne, it would become Protestant.

Often Mary would send for her sister and question her. Elizabeth feared that if she disagreed with Mary she might again be imprisoned in the Tower, and even beheaded. On one of these occasions Elizabeth threw herself on her knees before Mary, praying that the earth might open and swallow her alive if she were not a true Catholic.

Elizabeth was twenty-five when news was brought to her at Hatfield that Queen Mary was dead.

Immediately all the chief nobles and Ministers of the Crown came to pay allegiance to Elizabeth. The heralds blew their trumpets and on a scarlet and gold platform before the gates of Hatfield House, proclaimed her Queen Elizabeth of England.

The new Queen's first act was to make her adviser, William Cecil, Secretary of State. For the next forty years he was Elizabeth's surest friend and wisest counsellor.

Elizabeth's return to London was a triumphal procession all the way. The people of England were tired of the persecutions of Mary's reign, and the Bishops and the Lord Mayor and Sheriffs of London came out to meet her, glorious in their colourful robes of office.

The hopes of the people of England were high when the young Queen was crowned at Westminster. They were fully justified. Before she died, England was to become rich and powerful as never before.

Elizabeth was now Queen of England. In those days, England and Scotland were two separate kingdoms, and there was also a young Queen in Scotland. She was called Mary, Queen of Scots, and was Elizabeth's cousin.

Many people thought that Mary, Queen of Scots, ought to have been made Queen of England instead of Elizabeth. Mary was however a Catholic, and most of the English people wanted a Protestant Queen.

Mary herself claimed the throne of England, although she was married to the young King of France, as well as being Queen of Scotland in her own right.

Elizabeth was of course determined that Mary should never take the Crown of England away from her. Then the King of France died, and on a cold day of fog and rain, Mary returned to Scotland.

Elizabeth's rival was now her neighbour, north of the River Tweed.

Although Mary claimed the throne of England, she was much too occupied in trying to rule Scotland to take any steps to secure it.

For Mary was only nineteen years old when she returned from France, and she found that the Scots were far from being a quiet, peaceful people, easy to govern. The powerful Scottish nobles were always fighting one another, and were not prepared to obey a young Queen.

Mary did many things which made the Scottish people dislike her. She married a man named Lord Darnley who was very unpopular. When he was killed in an explosion, she became the wife of Lord Bothwell, who was suspected of having caused Darnley's death.

The Scottish people rose in arms against her, and Mary and Bothwell gathered their friends to resist them. The two armies met at a place called Langside, and Mary's friends were beaten and scattered. Mary fled across the Solway Firth into England.

Mary was now at the mercy of Queen Elizabeth. As she had tried to take the throne of England away from her, Mary could expect little mercy, even though Elizabeth was her cousin.

The Queen of Scots was lodged in Carlisle Castle and word was sent to Elizabeth in London. Mary hoped that the Queen would receive her kindly, and might even help her to get back her throne in Scotland.

Elizabeth, however, had not forgotten that Mary had plotted against her. Instead of letting her come to London and receiving her as a Queen, she had Mary arrested and kept in a castle in the North of England.

Then some of the noblemen in Northumberland and Westmorland raised an army and tried to set Mary free. They intended to make her Queen of England, but they were beaten and driven out of the country and Mary was kept more closely guarded than before. For nearly twenty years she remained a prisoner in England.

There are still old inns in England to-day which were built in the time of Queen Elizabeth. In many of them Elizabeth herself must have eaten and slept, for she was a great traveller, and was always moving from one part of the country to another.

We can imagine the scene when Elizabeth arrived at an inn in some market town. The soldiers and nobles who accompanied and guarded her would be wearing wonderfully coloured uniforms and clothes of brocade and silk, but the Queen would be more magnificent than any of them. Elizabeth loved gorgeously decorated dresses and rich jewellery.

The landlord would be bowing under the inn sign. The common people would be pressing forward to see the show and, smiling, beautiful and gracious, would be the young Queen herself, Elizabeth of England.

The reign of Elizabeth was a time of adventurous deeds at sea. The sailors of England made wonderful voyages in their little sailing ships and discovered many new lands.

Of all the men who sailed from our shores into unknown seas, the greatest was Sir Francis Drake.

The Spaniards had discovered the rich lands of South America and their ships were bringing cargoes of gold back to Spain. They did not want anyone else to get any of this gold, so they tried to prevent ships from other countries from sailing the South Atlantic Ocean, which they called the Spanish Main.

But Drake was not afraid of the Spaniards and he sailed his ship wherever he pleased. Although England was not at war with Spain, he attacked and burnt their settlements and sank their ships wherever he found them.

Sir Francis Drake was the first English-man to sail round the world.

He sailed from Plymouth on a winter's day in the year 1577. His ship was named the "Pelican", but before he returned to England, three years later, he had re-named it the "Golden Hind". It is a name which will never be forgotten so long as English ships sail the seas.

Drake crossed the Atlantic, capturing a Portuguese ship as he did so. Arriving at the coast of South America he attacked several Spanish settlements, taking much gold and silver.

Then he sailed on, far to the south and into the Pacific, still attacking and capturing Spanish ships and towns.

Now he had to decide how to get back to England. He tried to sail round the north of America, but was stopped by the ice. So he sailed westward, and after rounding the Cape of Good Hope, he returned home.

As a reward for his great voyage, he was knighted by the Queen on the deck of his ship.

Drake was only one, although the greatest, of the sailors of Elizabethan England.

Sir Walter Raleigh was another whose name we honour. Although, like Drake, he was ready to fight the Spaniards wherever he found them, he thought that instead of destroying Spanish settlements, it would be better to found English ones.

Raleigh thought more of the future greatness of England than he did of getting rich. So when he sailed to the New World, as America was then called, he took with him men who were ready to stay there and build houses and towns.

This was not easy. Often they had to fight with the Red Indians, and more than once their houses were burnt and many of them killed. But they were not disheartened, and the State of Virginia in America still bears the name of the colony they founded.

The English sailors were right to attack the Spaniards at sea or on land, because Philip of Spain was always plotting against England.

Then a new plot was discovered. An Englishman named Babington planned to kill Elizabeth and to make Mary Queen of England. To do this he arranged with Philip that when Elizabeth was dead, a Spanish Army should come and occupy England.

All this was arranged very secretly. Letters were sent to Mary hidden in barrels of wine, and she agreed to the plot.

Elizabeth had a very clever Minister called Walsingham, and he knew everything that was going on. So just when Babington and his friends were ready to carry out the plot, he had them arrested and executed.

Mary, Queen of Scots, was equally guilty of this attempt on the life of Elizabeth. For this reason she, too, was executed.

The failure of the plot made Philip even more angry with England. He decided that the time had come to attempt the conquest of these islands, and he began to build ships and to raise a great army.

The sailors of England knew what Philip was doing. In the ports of Spain more and more ships were getting ready to sail against England. Sir Francis Drake decided to attack first.

He chose the Spanish port of Cadiz, and with a squadron of English ships he carefully sounded his way into the harbour.

The Spanish sailors were not expecting to be attacked, and when Drake's ships suddenly appeared out of the darkness, they deserted their ships and made for the shore.

So Drake was able to burn 10,000 tons of shipping. This he called "singeing the King of Spain's beard".

But the building of ships went on in the Spanish harbours and soon a great fleet was ready to sail against England. It was called the Armada.

In England preparations were made to defend the country. On hill-tops from south to north great bonfires were built, and by night and day men stood ready to flash the signal from hill to hill when the Armada was sighted.

Soldiers were gathered at Tilbury and here the Queen made a speech to them, every word of which should be remembered. This is what Queen Elizabeth said:

" I know I have but the body of a weak and feeble woman; but I have the heart of a King, and of a King of England, too; and I think foul scorn that Spain, or any Prince of Europe, should dare to invade the borders of my realms. I myself will be your general, and I doubt not we shall shortly have a famous victory over the enemies of my God, of my kingdom, and of my people".

The Armada sailed from Spain and was sighted by Drake, who was playing a game of bowls on Plymouth Hoe. Drake looked at the Spanish sails to seaward and turned back to the green.

"There is time to win the game and beat the Spaniards too", he said calmly.

The Armada sailed slowly up the Channel, but it was not left long to sail in peace. From a score of English ports the English ships put out to sea. They were all smaller than the Spanish ships, but they were commanded by men like Drake, Hawkins, Frobisher and Lord Howard of Effingham.

What was more important, they were lighter and swifter and lower in the water than the Spanish ships. This enabled them to sail in under the enemy's guns, fire a broadside, and slip away without damage.

This they continued to do all that day, until the flagship of the Spanish Admiral Oquendo blew up.

When the Spanish sailors tried to get alongside the English ships, so that they could jump on board and capture them, the English were too quick for them. Over and over again they fired their guns into the hulls of the Spanish ships and darted away unharmed.

Then the wind dropped, and both fleets were becalmed. The Spaniards thought this was the end of the battle, but they did not know Francis Drake.

Seeing a great Spanish ship motionless on the water, a little behind the others, he sent boat-loads of sailors to capture it. The Spanish guns could not be pointed down to fire on the rowing boats, so the English sailors fastened ropes to the big ship and towed it away, with all its officers and sailors on board.

The fighting began again, and soon the Spaniards knew that they were beaten. When a favourable wind sprang up, all the Spanish ships which remained sailed into Calais harbour.

They were not left undisturbed. As soon as darkness fell, Drake ordered some old ships to be filled with oil and tar and anything that would burn. Then he set fire to them and sent them drifting to where the Spanish ships were all clustered together at anchor.

When the Spaniards saw a line of blazing ships floating towards them they tried desperately to escape. Some collided in the darkness. Others ran aground. But many of them managed to get away to sea.

These sailed away northwards, continuously attacked, until none of the English ships had any powder and shot left.

Then the weather changed and a great storm blew up from the south-west. There was only one thing the Spaniards could do, that was to try to return to Spain by sailing round the North of Scotland.

Westerly gales drove many of the ships on to the rocky coasts of Scotland and Ireland, and less than half of the famous Armada, broken, battered, and beaten, returned to Spain.

The great Armada was defeated, but English sailors continued to attack Spanish ships at sea wherever they could find them.

Sir Richard Grenville was one of the Elizabethan sailors who will always be remembered for his last great fight against the Spaniards.

In his ship, the "Revenge", he was surrounded by Spanish galleons, all of them larger and with more cannon than the little English vessel. The Spaniards opened fire, and all through the long day the guns roared. Shot for shot the "Revenge" returned their fire, until her masts were shot away, her rudder disabled, and her hull torn and shattered.

Still the "Revenge" fought on. Half the crew were killed and the rest wounded. Sir Richard Grenville was stricken and dying, and as he lay on the deck he commanded the master gunner to blow up the ship rather than surrender.

Suddenly the Spanish guns ceased to fire. The Spaniards were brave men and honoured bravery. As Sir Richard Grenville died they stood in silence with lowered flags, in tribute to a gallant enemy.

The reign of Elizabeth has been called the Golden Age of English Literature. This means, that as well as the great sailors and explorers, there were living at that time men who wrote some of the most wonderful poems and plays in our language.

Among these was a man named Spenser, who wrote a long and very beautiful poem called "The Faerie Queene".

This poem was written when Spenser was living in Ireland, where he had the good fortune to meet with one of the Queen's favourites, Sir Walter Raleigh. When he heard Spenser read the early books of this long poem, Raleigh decided to take Spenser to England and present him to the Queen.

Elizabeth was very fond of poetry and was delighted with "The Faerie Queene". Spenser became a regular visitor at the Court and was granted a pension.

A far greater man than Edmund Spenser was William Shakespeare, the greatest of all poets and playwrights.

Shakespeare was born in Stratford-upon-Avon, in one of the most beautiful parts of England, but he had to leave it because, so it is said, he had been killing the deer on the estate of one of the rich men of the district.

So he went to London and soon found work in one of the theatres. These were very unlike the theatres of to-day. They had platforms instead of stages, and they were open to the sky.

The theatres were under the protection of the Queen and the great nobles, and soon the plays which Shakespeare wrote for the Globe Theatre attracted the notice of Elizabeth herself.

The Queen liked Shakespeare's plays so much that he was frequently commanded to bring his company to the palace. It is wonderful to think that many of the plays which we see to-day were first acted before the great Queen Elizabeth herself.

The sailors of Elizabeth's reign did not sail only to the New World. Some explored new ways to the East, where they found India and China, with their ancient civilisations and great riches. The stories which these sailors brought back made people realise that much money might be made by trading with the Orient.

When Elizabeth came to the throne England was a poor country. All through her reign she had tried to make it richer, sometimes by capturing treasures from the Spaniards, and sometimes by encouraging trade overseas.

Here was another opportunity. The Court of the Mogul at Delhi was one of the richest in the world. So Elizabeth sent an Englishman, Sir John Mildenhall, to arrange for trade between England and India.

As a result of his visit, the East India Company was formed. This was one of the greatest trading companies of all time.

Queen Elizabeth had many favourites amongst the nobles and gentlemen who made up her Court, and chief amongst these was Robert Devereux, Earl of Essex.

Essex was not a great statesman or a very wise general, and when he was unsuccessful in Ireland the Queen recalled him to England in disgrace. This made Essex so angry that he tried to raise the citizens of London against the Queen's ministers, whom he accused of influencing her against him.

The attempt was unsuccessful. Essex was arrested, imprisoned in the Tower, and condemned to be beheaded.

When Essex was in favour with Elizabeth, she had given him a ring, and told him that if ever he should be in danger, he had only to send it to her, and she would save him. He sent it now, but it came into the hands of the Countess of Nottingham, who hated Essex, and the Queen never received it.

Essex was beheaded in the Tower, and it was only when it was too late, that Elizabeth discovered how Lady Nottingham had betrayed him.

Queen Elizabeth reigned over England for forty-five years. When she came to the throne England was poor. When she died, England was rich, prosperous, united and happy.

Her reign saw the beginnings of what came to be the British Empire. The fighting sailors of her reign, and the great victory over the Spanish Armada, made England one of the greatest of the countries of Europe.

Much of this was due to the character of Elizabeth herself. She never despaired and she never gave in.

It was reported that when she was very ill, King James of Scotland, who was to be the next King of England, sent one of his nobles to see how ill she was. Although she could hardly stand she dressed in her finest clothes and took part in a dance in his presence.

She died a few days later.

Series 561